The Hen Party

Sharon Cote

authorHOUSE®

AuthorHouse™
1663 Liberty Drive, Suite 200
Bloomington, IN 47403
www.authorhouse.com
Phone: 1-800-839-8640

First published by AuthorHouse 11/18/2008

ISBN: 978-1-4389-0405-4 (sc)

Printed in the United States of America
Bloomington, Indiana

This book is printed on acid-free paper.

Preface

I have written this book as kind of an insight for people. The topics that I wrote about are things we deal with on a regular basis. These are things that people see, live, hear, and speak of on a day-to-day basis, and although they are things we have to face every day, people either brush them aside or don't validate the importance of the knowledge we all have within. This book is not only a dedication to people but a validation as well, because for each page you read you will see a resemblance in either your life or the life of someone you know.

Everything in this book is information I've gathered from hen parties I attended, or sitting in a restaurant, listening to people, or working in a bar, or even getting an oil change. This is knowledge from my experiences in life, but also other people's experiences. Although we have all had similar but different experiences, they are all helpful in one way or another.

Although I may look at things or situations one way, you probably look at them another, and by people sharing, it helps others to either cope or change their situation. So I decided to put my stuff on paper, so that maybe it can help someone with a dilemma, situation, or an experience that they are having difficulty with.

This book is not only a tribute to people and their individualism, but it is filled with knowledge that I have gathered from people such as you. With that being said, I would like to thank all of the people who have touched my life in one way or another. Yes, even those people who made things not-so-great, because it was through those experiences that I've been able to improve myself as a person, friend, and confidant. I would like to thank the people who gave me joy, memories that I will cherish as well.

So here's to all the people, not just a chosen few. I thank you for your support with my writing, and hope that I have given you as much insight as you have given me. So sit back and enjoy, and hopefully you'll talk to me, as well as laugh and realize with me as you continue with your reading.

I would, however, like to give my sister Dorothy special thanks for all of her encouragement in this, because really, if it wasn't for her I would not be doing this today. She has helped me to get past my fears and do the things I would like to do, so here's to you Sis. Thanks from the bottom of my heart.

The Hen Party

This is a function where women get together and talk. The name "hen party" was created by men, but what they don't realize is that it was probably one of these parties that helped save their marriage at one time or another.

Yes, when women get together, they talk about everything, such as their marriages, relationships, children, and families. Women tend to talk about whatever is bothering them the most. Even though women like to say it's an opportunity to get away and to see how everyone is doing and what they're doing, women use each other as sounding boards, and yes, there's a whole lot of counseling going on that they don't even realize. They use each other to help with the dilemmas in their relationships, children, and even their workplace; it's a safe way for them to vent.

Even though a man may feel the parties are a total waste of time, he's wrong, because at one of those meetings his wife may have been having a problem with him, and the other women helped sort it out. She feels better and goes home with a whole new outlook on the situation. So men, instead of trying to prevent these little parties, you should embrace them, because it does make your life a lot easier. I'm not saying that you don't have to do your part; I'm just saying that this makes it easier to do.

It's truly amazing what a group of women can accomplish without even realizing it. Unfortunately these parties grow less and less frequent because of women's busy schedules, but when they finally find the time, look out, because holy cow! The talk could last all night.

Women feel comfortable in that atmosphere because it's helpful, and they realize they aren't the only one with those kinds of problems. However, men feel insecure at the parties because they feel that the other women are going to tell his woman something negative, when in fact, 80 percent of the time it's very positive and helps the woman face another day. I always say that if men would only do the same thing we'd all be better off. But that's highly unlikely to ever happen, because men bottle their emotions and true feelings up and women don't, so that is why the parties are so helpful.

This is not about slamming men; it's about why these parties happen. If they read this, maybe the men won't be so insecure when their wives or girlfriends say "I'm going to see the girls tonight," because it's only going to help.

Men and women obviously handle things differently. That is why we have books like *Men Are from Mars, Women Are from Venus*, but communication is actually easier than people make it out to be. Like women venting with each other, keeping communication as open as it was at the beginning of the relationship and making sure that each person knows the silent expectations decided at the dating stage of the game still has to continue throughout the rest of the relationship. Isn't this something we are all guilty of at one time or another in a relationship?

Hen parties aren't just a place to vent, but are also good for the soul. They help to relive accomplishments in one's life and help with new accomplishments; they give new ideas; they are confidence seminars without the stuffy seminar; they let others know that they are not alone with anything, and the support system is there. The parties help visions become realities because of the strong support system involved in these groups.

Believe it or not, hen parties help women conquer any problems they may have and put a whole new outlook on each individual's life. So for me, I am extremely grateful for the parties I've attended, and I miss them every day, especially when I'm going through a difficult time. They have always helped me with my dilemmas.

So, always value hen parties no matter what anyone says, because there will be a time in your life when you don't have that team to depend on, and you'll realize how valuable they were.

People

The story I've written is about people. It is about all the things we think we have lost and all the things we know deep inside. I wrote this story because I feel that we, as people, are getting a raw deal. I am hoping to help people remember why we are different from the animal kingdom, and that to be different is not entirely a bad thing.

This story is a salute to all those individuals out there that tend to forget why we are who we are as the days go by.

I'm hoping that in my writings people will know that even in today's society of "It's a dog-eat-dog world" we may be part of the animal kingdom, but we are still human beings. We still have some of the old beliefs and values that once was, and it's not a bad thing.

I feel that the things that I have written about help readers remember another famous saying: "That people seemed to have lost touch with who they really are and what they're all about." I'm hoping that my writings will help people realize these things and maybe to get some of that back.

However, though I have not said all that could be said on this topic, I feel I have expressed the parts that hit home the most.

This book is about people, it is about all the individuals that make up the world today. It ranges from young to old, poor to middle class, middle class to upper middle class, and from middle class to rich. It covers all the people, not just one specific group.

Now, I'm not a psychiatrist, psychologist, sociologist, or anyone else who studies human nature. I am just a regular person who in her lifetime seems to have found the study of people to be quite exciting. All the jobs I have ever done always involved people, and I seem to make it a habit to watch people on a regular basis.

I can remember my dad telling me at the supper table not to stare at people, but what I was actually doing was studying them and their movements and actions, which I still do today. I probably will for a very long time, because I find individuals fascinating. There is so much to be learned, it's unbelievable.

I come from a family of all girls, five to be exact, and of course in our lives we've all taken different paths. Like my older sister, for example. She is very book smart and always has been; you could put her under the heading of that which I said I was not, because she has had the educational training for it. Even though I have not had the same training as her, I have had training from the School of Life, which for the most part can be quite challenging.

This sister that I spoke of is part of the reason why I am putting these thoughts out to you. She had been sending me some inserts on different topics, and most of those topics are about behavioral patterns, why people do some of the things they do, and what part of their emotional states plays a part in it. To my great surprise, she asked me for my input. So I wrote her back, giving her my insight into some of the inserts that she sent, and my other sister read what I wrote, and she said maybe you should write a book. As I was travelling to my new job, I thought about what it was that my sister said and started thinking about all the things I felt. I said to her in our conversation that people are losing their individualities, that with all the surveys and states that are out there, it's taking the individuality out of people. I asked her where we would be without individuals; after all, it was individuals who gave us some of the things that we cherish. So I decided to put my thoughts on paper and let people know that it's not fair that everything that we are about should be put down in number form, so this is actually a book about people and giving them praise for their individuality.

I've gathered quite a bit of information over the last twenty to thirty years to do with this. You see, I'm a watcher; I like to watch people, the things they do, the gestures they make, and of course the things they say.

I was a stay-at-home mom for many years, so I became very nosy; now if I go anywhere with anyone, or even by myself, I watch people. Sometimes I get so caught up in it I forget about the person I'm with. They'll always ask "Do you have to do that?" and I'll say yes, because people are fascinating. Then I'll tell them what's going on around us and they're amazed. And that's all because of people.

As I was saying, the jobs that I've had over the last number of years included dealing with people either in employee forms or customer form. Either way it has been quite fascinating. Over the years I've met some incredible people and some I thought were not so incredible at the time. However, I found that over time as I got to know these people that they were as incredible, if not more so than the people I thought were at the start. You know, the saying "You can't judge a book by its cover" is so true. I have found over the years that some people put this big front on to make people believe they are not exactly who they really are, and that is done so they aren't at risk for them to get hurt either emotionally or financially. I know this because I am one of those people, and I see it every day. So those people usually test the waters with the person standing in front of them, and then when they get comfortable they let their guard down and you get to experience the real person inside of them.

Let's touch on relationships a little. Most women are natural caregivers, and most men are natural protectors. For the most part women take care of the home, men, and children; they are the rocks of emotion, the deciders of the right and wrong of things. Whereas most men make sure that the people in their homes have the material and financial things they need. But sometimes women have to be like men in the way they are not only the caregivers but the financial winners as well, depending on the circumstances (e.g., single moms, widows).

But men only have to check their emotions when it is necessary, such as if the woman discovers that she's not entirely happy with her situation, the man will always say the right things to make her think twice, and she will decide to stay and work on things a bit more. Then every time she has questions after that, he always says or does something that makes it different from the time before, and woman concedes to the man. So the man stays happy, secure, and in charge in that way. But there is a lesson to be learned for women; it is the lesson of how he can do that every time and how he does it, and the lesson for men is to learn that emotions cannot be a damaging thing but a good thing. The man doesn't have to come up with just the right thing to say at his time of need if he had only said something once in a while. It helps to prevent the inevitable.

So if you haven't noticed already I'm going to jump around a little, or maybe even a lot, that's because there is so much to say on this matter, and as the thoughts flow I put them down, so please bear with me. There will always be something you can relate to, or at least I hope there will be.

I spoke earlier of my dad and the fact he didn't like me looking around, especially at the dinner table. But I've come to the realization that by him telling me not to do that he was creating tunnel vision, and to be quite honest I'm glad that I chose not to listen. I might have gotten into a lot of trouble because of it, but it's all been worth it because I have been able to experience people at their finest, and of course at their worst. It's because of all the individuals out there that I've been able to look at some of my situations differently than if I had followed his teachings.

I have also noticed through the years that people are more inclined to go with the majority than to step out of their shell and take a chance. I find that if you step out of what you find to be your comfort zone than it leaves you open to some realities that you may not want to take. I've done the same every so often. But then I realize that life is too short, and sometimes you have to take that chance to really get what you want or to even experience others and what they might want. Sometimes it works out and sometimes it doesn't, but then how are we ever going to learn anything without stepping out once in a while? You know these things happen because of society today and the beliefs it has put on everyone.

When we go for help with purchasing a car, house, home improvements, or just some financial relief, we are all put in the same categories by the institutions that we helped create. For example, I'm sure you've heard or know someone who's heard "I'm sorry, but you don't fit the criteria" even if you've done nothing to fit the criterion, such as gotten a loan or built credit in one way or another, but how are you suppose to fit the criterion when you are not able to get a chance to do that? Years ago, people were looked at on an individual basis when they wanted to do something to improve their situation, and now everyone is looked at the same when we know not everyone is the same, but society tells us we are. That's like the saying "Do as the Joneses do" It's all just a matter of labeling, and only we can change that because we're the ones who made it that way.

This book is a tribute to all the individuals out there who help someone cross the street, who give flowers to their wife, girlfriend, friend, mother, sister, or father. It's a salute to someone helping in a car crash, helping a child succeed, or visiting the elderly, giving someone a compliment, or giving their seat up on a bus for someone else. This is to all the individuals out there that make the world what it is today.

This book is to say thanks to all individuals for helping make my bad days good, for making me realizing my life isn't so bad, for helping me experience all the emotions that we all store deep inside. This book is to say thanks for letting me know chivalry still exists.

I'm hoping that my writings help people think twice the next time they say or think "they're all the same," or "they'll do anything to get what they want," or "Isn't there anymore good in this world today?" Hopefully my writings help people to remember that not everyone is the same and that no matter who we are or what we say or do, there is always something good that can come from it.

Hopefully my writings help relieve someone of the thought "Will things ever turn around?" or "Why does that person have to be that way?" Just remember, things happen to people that make them who they are, and although they may not have been that way before, something happened to make them that way now.

Remember that there is no such thing as a small or large accomplishment, just that you were able to accomplish it.

As I've said previously, I've watched people all my life, and I'll probably watch them for the rest of my life. I find individuals to be extraordinary people. Just when we think society has turned their back, or maybe it's even gone to the dogs, one individual will change that for us. That's what's so interesting, that there is always something around the corner to change our mind or to make us think twice.

I also find that a lot of people talk about things they did in their past—things they accomplished and things they got praise for. Most of that is because it is those thoughts that keep us going through difficult times. I know, I know, when someone does that repeatedly the saying is "Can't they talk about anything else?" or "I've heard this over and over again," or "Here we go again, living in the past," but those are memories, and those are things we like to hold on to. After all, nobody wants to tell anybody of their defeats or the disaster in the workforce, or the reprimand they received, because that's all negative. We usually repeat their stories or sometimes apply something they've said to something we do or say. It's our nature to take something good or bad someone did or said and make it ours, in order to make us feel better, and to strive at what it is we are trying to get or do.

But sometimes we need to hear about the negative experiences of others and find out how they got through them so we can apply it in our lives. People are funny that way. They would never admit to taking that particular information and using it to their advantage.

I always say that if people who have been married for twenty-five years and up would talk more about the bad parts of their marriages, ours today would last a lot longer. Because then maybe we could apply the knowledge of these past troubles to our own and not give up so easily.

Remember the things we find most annoying are the things we remember the most. Such as those ridiculous commercials, or maybe something someone said or did. That's what you'll remember, not the phone number on the TV that may help you in an area you need help, and not the inspiring statement someone gave you, but the thing that drove you crazy with frustration. And then later you'll discover: "Oh my God, I can't believe I did that myself or used that!" because you found it so annoying at the time it happened, but you did get enough out of it to apply it to yourself and your circumstances. So do you see what I mean by people are amazing? There is always at least one person who says or does one thing that so many others can learn from.

That is why I'm writing this book, so people don't get lost in the shuffle. All the things we used to know and do that were exciting to us are slowly disappearing, and because we pour our hearts and souls into most everything we do, they are disappearing with it. So the one thing you did that made you that individual just went by the wayside. So remember, you are still an individual, and you also have the ability to do something else to keep it that way.

There are so many things I haven't touched on and pointed out, so remember this: For as long as you keep your tunnel vision or blinders on, you will never get to experience the finer things in your life or others.

Remember, from one common person to another we were all common people at one time. For those who haven't experienced what someone down your family tree did and they are why you are who you are today, it is because they did something you did that would stop you from being in a harder place as they were at one time.

So treat everyone as the individual they are, and not a number on a list. Every so often we need a little push, such as the person who did the smiley face or even the Pet Rock, and all those who write fairy tales. Those were all crazy or unrealistic ventures that took help from others, but as it turned out they all were good and prosperous ventures. So remember yours, remember that they are not so farfetched that they can't become realities as well.

I would like to thank my sister Dorothy for her kind words and thoughts. For if it wasn't for her saying what she felt at the time, I would not have done this today.

Relationships

Most women are natural caregivers. Most men are natural protectors. For the most part women take care of the men, home, and children. They are the rocks of emotion, and the deciders of the right and the wrong of things. Whereas most men make sure that the people in the home have the material things they need to be satisfied and feel safe.

What amazes me is all of the work both men and woman have to do to get to the point of having the perfect family and marriage and being comfortable with what they have. But what most people don't realize is that the comfort is what can take it all away.

In relationships we have different levels of comfort with each other; it's a process, the longer you're with someone, of course the greater the comfort. And in that comfort comes forgetfulness. People tend to forget all the things they did to attract that individual to them. The things they did to keep the attraction. Specifically the little things like noticing a new hairdo, a new outfit, giving a hug, a kiss on the cheek for no reason, going dancing regularly (if you dance), feeling pride and showing it to others when the person is with them, going for dinner, and that's just a few. I know a lot of these things are centered toward the woman and her needs, and that's true, but that's how it all starts. Now everyone wants their relationships to be 50/50, and in the dating stages you can have that, but as soon as marriage hits, it changes somewhat.

The beginning of a relationship is of course dating and you have around 80/20 effort on the man's side, because they are working so hard to get the woman's attention. That is how it goes; the man has to work harder to get the one he wants.

But what people don't realize is that women automatically start taking the 80% on themselves by the things they do, such as making the man feel like he's king of the castle.

Then we get to the living together stage, and she takes charge again. This happens with women instinctively. They cook the meals, do the laundry, clean the house, pay attention to his every need, and give him everything he wants and needs without him saying a word. A woman will even go as far as changing jobs or quitting a job, she will even step down from their business if they have one together, just so she can get at home to help him be successful at whatever he chooses to do. The man, on the other hand, instinctively goes into king role, where he makes most of the money, fixes things around the house, takes care of the vehicle maintenance and sometimes says I love you, and occasionally gives a compliment or takes his girl out for a night on the town (so to speak). Although the woman does things constantly to make the man feel good and secure, the man only does things periodically. This can cause questions for the woman, such as "Does he still love me? Am I still attractive to him?" or "What have I done for it to be so different from when we were dating?"

The only thing the woman wants in return is an action of verification of her man of his love for her. It really is that simple. People just make it difficult.

It's like when a person other than your wife such as your common-law or your girlfriend does something for you, you do something in return to show your appreciation. That is how a relationship should work. Because all we need is that feeling of gratification, verification, and a sense of doing something meaningful for someone we love.

That leads us back to the comfort zone. Women make men comfortable throughout their relationship at the cost of time for themselves, because they are always thinking of and doing things to make sure the man feels that way. It is then left up to the man to reciprocate, which unfortunately doesn't always happen. This causes women to start questioning their relationships and whether or not their man loves them anymore. So when she feels that way she talks to her man and he tells her everything she needs to hear for her to feel differently. Unfortunately, though, they do not always show it as well. The key is not so much the words but the actions. Whereas at the start of the relationship he was all action, but somewhere along the way it got lost.

So, all in all, do actions speak louder than words?

Most of the time in relationships when a woman starts to question herself and how her man feels toward her, she lets herself go. For example, she may not do her hair, not wear make-up, gain weight, or change the clothes she wears. Then the man starts to lose the attraction, and feels that she is no longer the woman he was attracted to, and definitely not the same woman he married. Then a light bulb goes on for the woman and she starts to change those things, which causes the man to think that there is someone else, because she's back to her old self. This all causes needless problems in the relationship. If the man had just kept doing later in the relationship what he done in the beginning, none of this would have happened.

After all, the words you'll hear from almost every woman are "I just want the man that I thought I married." It is really that simple. Everyone lets themselves go a little in a relationship, and that's the healthy part of a comfort zone. It's when it goes too far that it does damage. Where they say "I just don't care anymore," and that is getting into the unhealthy comfort zone.

Women just want the man that made them feel special, beautiful, like they could talk and tell them anything, to make them feel intelligent and like a real woman. That's all, and if the men do that during the relationship as well as at the start, then you have a beautiful thing. But once that comes to an end, it means an end to the relationship as well, because that factors in the loss of what was once a great thing.

Communication in relationships is not just words spoken but actions taken as well. You can tell someone everyday you love them, but unless you show it physically and materialistically it leaves room for question. The only way women are really complicated is if she has to question her femininity. No questions, no problems. It is that simple.

Now, although this may not apply to all relationships, it does apply depending on who feels more comfortable and who is giving less.

I know these things because I've seen them, just not in my own but in others lives, and the one thing I'll say to the man I'm with is that the comfort zone is a bad place because these things I mentioned are exactly what happens. So remember, you do have to work as hard to keep someone as you did to get them, and if you didn't work that hard in the first place there will be a time where you'll have to work even harder. It is the little things in life that give us the most pleasure, and if you don't have that, then you will always be looking for it. And that pretty much is verification that you mean as much to the person five to twenty years later as they did the first day you started your process, and in this case *actions do speak louder than words.* So take the work out of your relationship and put the job back in.

Now, I realize that there are other problems that come up in marriages, the biggest one being money. But the main problem is of what I spoke of, and because of the main problem we always find other things to argue about, because the main problem is the unspoken part, and that part comes up when two people are parting. You have to remember that the marriages that have lasted twenty, thirty, or forty years all had money issues as well, plus these main problems, but they worked it out by treating each other the way I spoke of. Back then, you dealt with things in marriage, and you didn't get divorced, you toughed it out. But now divorce is the easy solution. So why create a solution to a problem when you don't have to have the problem to begin with?

So remember, the only way for a relationship to be really 50/50 is if both parties show actions as well as spoken words.

It really is that simple.

Habits

Let's talk about habits, shall we? A habit can be a security blanket. This can in turn cause an addiction, which then creates predictability and expectations.

First an example habit: A person goes to one specific restaurant regularly, such as every day at the same time; they always drink and eat the same thing. That person's actions cause predictability, which can in turn affect other people. Most habits can't, won't, or should not be broken. When someone is secure with what they do and where they go every day, it gives them a sense of security. They know that there is a definite thing in their life, and no matter how messed up the rest of their day goes, they always have that. People go to restaurants at different certain times of the day, the times most common are breakfast and supper. Lunch is not included because it's midday, and where you go it is often dependent on where you work and with whom you are going. But breakfast and supper is kind of their own time, to either plan their day or just relax from it. Now, at this restaurant they also always sit at the same table and have the same waitress. So when someone goes to the same place at the same time and eats, drinks, and sits at the same table, it creates predictability, because after a while the waitress starts watching for that person and starts getting their stuff ready for them, and after a while when they see that person come in they'll put their order in before they even sit down. And if that person changes what they always have after a while, that can cause disruption for the waitress and can actually throw her day off. Because waitresses tend to get dependant on their predictability, if that person doesn't show up for a week or two it can cause the waitress to worry as to whether or not something bad has happened to their customer. The only way to prevent the worry is to tell the waitress you won't be there because of a vacation or something else, which is not unreasonable because of the relationship and friendship that you both have formed. You tell each other all kinds of stuff about each of you, so that would not be unusual to tell her about your vacation plans. If the person doesn't have his daily ritual, though, then his whole day can be messed up and he'll think: "I know I should have done what I always do".

ADDICTION: Consider either being a social drinker or smoker; these two items are both very addicting. The social part could very easily turn into something more regular than you think. People don't realize it's happening until someone points it out. The people being told about it will always deny that they are doing either or both more often than they were, which leads to the addiction. After all, both habits are highly addicting, need I say more?

EXPECTATIONS: The ones I speak of have to do with the people whom you meet and get to know in the usual places you go. Seeing them every day at the same time doing the same things creates expectations of them, such as the waitress I spoke of earlier. They expect to see you there, and as I said if you're a no-show and they aren't aware that you won't be there, then they tend to worry, and it does affect them. I know this because I have been a waitress and have had regular customers, and I have been affected in the ways I spoke of earlier, such as when they weren't there at the time they always normally were.

Families

This is a story about families. It consists of all the good and bad about families—the things that we do to each other, and the things we give to each other. This story is going to end with the reasons we seem to forget why family is so important.

In this story I'm going to try to hit on all of the things that happen within the family unit. The things we discuss with friends, family members, and counselors. Throughout this story you will realize that there are more similarities within all types of people than you realize. Yes, believe it or not, even the wealthy have the same family problems as you or I do.

So remember, even though you think you're the only one dealing with things, there are thousands going through exactly what you are.

All the things I write about really happen; they are not scenarios. They are all based on real life experiences, from not only my own but lots of people I either spoke to, or yes overheard. As I've said already, I am very nosy.

So you are never as alone as you feel.

All families deal with deception, hate, greed, anger, money problems, being taken advantage of, jealousy, lying, separation, mistrust, and insecurities.

We also deal with admiration, love, unity, support, and pride. And lastly, we all deal with death of a loved one.

So I'm going to start with a quote, which is "You can't pick your family, but you can pick your friends, so pick them wisely". You'll find for every negative situation this saying will be spoken at least once, and believe me, it is so true sometimes.

As we are growing up we argue, fight with, or even tease our siblings or cousins, and we don't think anything of it, because that's just what we do. But would you believe that those behaviors can come back to bite us in the butt? Yes, believe it or not it can happen, and I know there are people out there that can relate to my statement.

All through our growing stages from five to eighteen years of age and sometimes even after that, our parents tell us we shouldn't tease people, pick on them, be mean, or any of that. But hey, we think, "What's the big deal? I'm only joking." Or maybe you thought they knew you were only joking. This goes on for years, and you always think the same thing, and then you reach adulthood and you find out from the person or people you did that to that they took it to heart. You still can't understand how they could have carried it for so many years. So you try to apologize for what you did or said, even if you don't remember everything. But it doesn't always help, and then maybe you have a similar experience and then you really understand and can really apologize for what it was you did or said. You are more aware, so you then start watching what you say and do to make sure that nobody feels that way again because of your actions.

What most people don't realize until it is sometimes too late is that words can be a nasty tool. Words affect people all their lives, and for some it's very hard to get over it. Not only that, but words affect not only one person but many. This happens because people they harm can get blasted for something they said when it's not so much as that as to the harm that was done from somebody else. So remember, what you say may not only affect one person, but it can affect thousands, depending on how many years it takes for the person to deal with what you said, and whether or not you help them with that by realizing what you did and letting them know you are truly sorry.

Now we'll talk about deception. That happens more when someone tells you a secret and you tell everyone. Now the person who told you the secret feels deceived, because you led them to believe that they could tell you anything and it would not be repeated, which also causes mistrust. So when a person is being accused of telling a secret, they usually tell you that they didn't think it would get back to the person it was said about because the person they told was their confidant.

You have to remember that for every confidant you have there is another confidant, and that's how that happens, so when somebody tells you something and actually asks you not to tell anyone, don't! That means even your confidant, so remember the saying "mum's the word" and don't tell a soul. If you live by that you will never have to worry about the mistrust issue happening to you, and it is definitely a good rule to live by. And if you are really unable to keep a secret—and there are people like that—then make sure you're never put in that position. Just say "No, I don't want to hear about it," it's much safer that way.

Now we touch on hatred. I feel that the word hate is used almost as much as the word Love. I know you may not agree with that statement, but think about it. Not only do we say "I hate you" or that, but when we see something we like we say "I love that" as well. Sometimes we even use them in the same sentence, such as "I really hate that, but oh man I love that." I realize you might think this is ridiculous, but think about it. The two strongest words for use of expression as to how you feel are used almost as much as the other. Where love is a positive expression, hate is a negative expression that can do a great deal of harm. For example, when you are in a heated discussion with the one you love and they say something you don't like, you might tell them that you hate them. Unfortunately, we use it more than once, and when the person says "You don't really mean that," you say "Yes I do," and walk away. Now that one little word has just truly devastated the one you love more than life. Ergo, the saying "You always hurt the one you love". We have these sayings for a reason, most of the time people take them to lightly, which none of us should do.

Yes, all these things I'm mentioning are things we might say or do to our mom, dad, sister, or brother. Sometimes our aunt, uncle, or cousin, because we all have one of those that we look up to and consider them like your second mom, dad, brother, or sister. So be careful what you say, your words are more effective than you think.

Now for jealousy, it comes from something that you really want that someone else in your family gets. Maybe the person you spend a lot of time with and look up to starts spending time with another family member, and then all kinds of problems come out of it. The worse thing is that most people don't realize that they are going through that emotion, and when someone says something people tend to deny it. When they realize that's exactly what they're feeling, then anger comes into play, but not so much with the other person as themselves. So remember to be aware of the Big Green Monster, and don't let it get the best of you. That is where most insecurities come from, and it can also cause separation. When jealousy rears its nasty head it can cause people to separate themselves from that individual, and this can create an empty feeling or feeling like there's a void in your life. Just remember that life is too short for all of that.

Now we talk about lying. Lying, as we all know happens when you want to evade the truth. It also happens when we're mad at someone and want to get them in trouble. This can be a result of jealousy or mistrust as well. I don't really need to go into jealousy causing this, but as for mistrust, that is when in some situations when someone breaks our trust we just want to pay them back (revenge) for doing that to us. They tell themselves they'll just tell a small lie and that's it. When it comes to lying, remember that "people will believe a lie before the truth," and that's because the "Truth hurts," so when you tell one lie it can lead to another and another. It is always better to be known as someone who tells the truth than as a pathological liar, which can happen if people aren't careful.

Oh now money, which is one of the biggest causes of problems within the family. I think I'm pretty safe in saying that at least 93% of the population would agree, if not 98%. Now we get to being taken advantage of. Now with this one it's usually one or two people within the family that it happens to, but most of the other members notice this is happening and it causes them to withdraw from the person(s) that does this so the same thing doesn't happen to them. It's just like the "freeloader" that everyone stays away from.

We'll talk a little more about separation. It is caused when either someone loses trust or they feel that they have been taken advantage of, especially having to do with lying and money issues. You see, when someone tells a lie, even if it's a white lie, it causes people to separate themselves, and not only does the one that feels that way, but the people in the family separate themselves from the one it's been centered around, especially when it involves a lie. For the most part people within the family will not go to the one that's been accused or other; they will keep it to themselves, but mostly they'll talk to other family members and then it gets blown way out of proportion. For example, we've all played the game where one person starts with a few words and tells another and it goes down the line, and by the time it reaches the end most of it isn't even what was originally said. That's pretty much what happens with a lie; it starts with the originator and by the time someone finally confronts the person it's about, it's blown way out of proportion and then it's an endless cycle. Because more times than not the person that it started from will either say "I didn't say that" or "Well that's what so and so told me". So do you see how separation can happen without someone even trying? If only someone would have actually spoken up it probably wouldn't have happened to begin with. So we definitely need to work on the communication skills.

There won't be much in the way of insecurities because basically the things I listed do not only cause it but make it worse. Because when everything happens, people get insecure about what they do and who they are.

I'm going to talk about something that everyone finds hard to talk about, but it's something we all need to do or know about, because it is always right there; you just never know when it will happen in your life.

The things that people will do or say are amazing in this respect. Most people experience anger, separation, unity, support, love, understanding, blame, forgiveness, greed, loneliness, doubt, relief, anxiety, depression, tolerance, obligation, fear, forgetfulness, etc.

How many emotions people experience depends on the circumstances. If someone who has been sick and in pain for a long time dies, the emotion people experience the most is relief, and that's because the person doesn't have to suffer any longer.

Now, if they pass away from either suicide or someone else taking their lives, that is totally different. When it comes to suicide, no one will ever feel relief. Their feelings usually turn to guilt. I say guilt because other than the shock people experience upon hearing about it, some feel guilt because either they spoke to the deceased the day of or the day before, or had even seen them, or maybe they were supposed to see or talk to him or her and they didn't because they were just too busy.

Now you have to understand I'm no counselor, psychiatrist, psychologist, or anyone else in that field. I am a person who has life experiences with people that have been faced with this tragedy. No matter how anyone feels when a life is taken from us earlier than we figure it should be, it is always a tragedy. That is how people put it as well. I realize everyone has their own opinion about it, but remember the saying "You don't know what happens behind closed doors." This pertains to people's lives in every aspect. People don't know exactly everything someone else is thinking or experiencing. It's nobody's fault, and it's not like people do this to ruin other people's lives. The victims just really feel that it's the only thing they can do. They may feel they've tried everything and nothing is either good enough, or it just doesn't work. They have lost their fight for life, but you should never judge if you've never been there. After all, we all get or have been judged at one time, and there will be a day that we are. So remember that everyone deserves the benefit of doubt, as you yourself may have experienced it, because I know that I have had that happen. I have judged, and because of that I too have been judged, so I try my hardest to live by these three sayings: "Never judge a book by its cover," "Everyone deserves the benefit of the doubt," and "Walk a mile in my shoes then you'll know why."

The other part of this is for someone killed by someone else. This is an experience of my own, and I am going to speak of it in hopes that it may give you a better understanding.

In 2003, my daughter's common-law spouse took her life. The relationship was very abusive, but it didn't matter what we said or did, she kept going back. He had three beautiful children that she helped raise, and out of the love she felt for the children, she kept going back. In 2003 he shot her. It is now 2008, and we are still in the court system over it.

When I found out, I was in shock. Then it was all over the news, and I couldn't understand why they were going to the extreme they were; at one point the news reporter chased us down the street, wanting an interview. I think I experienced almost every emotion I named earlier.

People were incredible, even the other reporters we dealt with. They were very respectful. The people in my community were excellent; one lady even took three days to come and give her condolences. When she realized it was my daughter, even thepeople in the community went into shock. As one lady said "I heard it on the news and felt really bad for the people, then I realized it was someone's daughter I knew and it was basically right in my backyard, which really changes things". Everyone was so supportive, it was incredible. The kids my daughter knew were unbelievable as well.

It was really at this time that I realized how amazing people really are, and how much they are willing to help. It was an extremely difficult time, and surprisingly enough even the people that only knew her for a few weeks were experiencing some of the emotions I listed, and even today they still experience some of those emotions they felt at the time it happened. The two most prominent emotions in that situation were anger and guilt. Anger because he took her from us and justice was taking so long, and guilt because what else could we have done to get her out of that situation? But with time and the support of family, friends, and victim services we got through it, and will get through the rest.

I will add that a lot of people have trouble with the fact they either didn't get to say goodbye and were not able to tell her they loved her. So the funeral for my daughter was like a tribute to her with some of her favorite music, and I gave everyone the opportunity to say goodbye. Nobody could say the words goodbye, but they were given the opportunity and that's what mattered, everyone felt much better because of it. So even though we want to say goodbye, nobody really does. One thing I tell everyone close to me is that I love them at the end of each conversation. That way they always know. It doesn't matter how long it's been since I have seen or spoken to them last. So remember, although people might feel hurt when you don't say I love you, you are the only one who may regret it in the end. And we all know regret is an emotion nobody likes or should have to deal with.

So no matter how mad or hurt you're feeling, always tell the ones you love that you love them, because you never know when you won't be able to anymore. I say this through experience, and it is something I definitely do now because I have lost a child and I also really can relate to someone when they say "A parent should never have to bury one of their children." Before I thought I understood, and now I really do. It is one of the worst feelings ever, but thank God for memories, because it sure does make things easier. So does talking about it, even if it's a stranger, it really does help. Remember, communication and talking are the most important parts of a sound mind, life, and most of all soul.

Yes, communication and talking are different. Communication is where you tell each other about your day, no matter how good it was. Talking is where you can tell them exactly how you feel; whether it's good or bad, it's better than none at all. The only way to get through everything I've written and will write about is to talk.

Speak of your feelings, because they are real and no matter what they will always be there, so help each other, listen, and hear what each person is saying.

During the time of dealing with not only my emotional roller coaster after my daughter passed away, I got to experience someone else's greed. Greed is a reaction to the emotion fear. In this I mean that when someone passes on we experience the fear of losing the memory of the person that passed way, so we feel we have to have some sort of keepsake to help keep that memory alive; whether it's pictures, clothing, ornaments, or jewelry. So people will actually argue and fight over the belongings of the deceased out of the fear that has overwhelmed them, and for the most part people don't even realize that they are behaving ill-mannered; all they can think of is having something to be able to remember that person by. Although this behavior can be very disturbing for some family members, that is the reality of it, and the realization is unfortunately that we all need something of that person to remember, because eventually people tend to forget. This is not totally wrong, because it just means that they were finally able to accept what has happened and got the closure that they needed.

Just a little something to add. My children all look alike, which sometimes has its ups and downs, but they're okay with it for the most part. Now what I told my kids at the time when they were dealing with the part of forgetting was "That they are more fortunate than others because they all look so much alike, and because of that they have a physical memory of her, so for them they could never forget their sister because they all look alike, and for that they should be grateful." Now I look quite a bit like one of my sisters, and every time there is a problem with the two of us I think of what I told my kids and am quite grateful for our likeness. Because no matter what, whether I'm not talking to her or she does pass on I will always have that, and for that I am grateful. I realize we all do forget sooner or later, and for me it will be later rather then sooner. So if you have a relative that you look similar to, be thankful, because it really is a blessing.

So now that we've gone through the negative, how about some positive to the whole family concept.

We'll first deal with the unity part of it. Unity normally comes from things that happen in a family such as birth, death, graduation, weddings, baptismal, reunions, pride, etc. It happens with any function that requires us to all to be together, and during quite a few of these functions people will put their issues behind them and attend, but usually when they're all said and done it goes back to normal. Go figure!

Pride, well there's not much to say on that because it stems from special occasions and the things I mentioned above, but more so with graduations from elementary, high school, post-secondary, and university educations. So basically anything to do with either getting your education or expanding on it.

Pride covers other accomplishments, such as first steps, catching the winning ball, scoring the winning home run or touchdown, the winning goal to WHL or NHL, to the first communion, first recital, etc. Pride and how much of it we have comes from our parents, to us, to our children. It is one of the many things that we pass down from generation to generation. Because not only can we feel pride in ourselves and our children, but our children might be able to have pride in us for our accomplishments, such as going back to school to finish that Bachelors degree, or just going back to school.

So sit back for a moment and think of your siblings and parents, and go ahead and put a smile on your face even if you're mad at them. Smile about the things they accomplished, and how they made you laugh when you really needed it. Now isn't that better? For a second you remembered exactly why you love them as you do, and isn't joy a much better feeling than all those bad feelings you felt a minute or so ago?

So really, that's what support is: it's being there in the good times and bad, no matter how angry, frustrated, or disgusted you may feel at one time or another. Even through all those emotions I mentioned you will once again show them the support they need, even if it's against your better judgment. You'll be there because that's all part of being a family.

Admiration is truly something that people have trouble with, but just think, you show a form of admiration every time you go to a graduation or wedding. Admiration is one emotion that is made up of a few, including love, support, and pride, because it takes all of those to attend these functions and say "I'm here because I want you to know I recognize your accomplishments." This is a form of admiration. Just like when an Alcoholic stays dry for many years or someone kicks a drug habit, etc. But with these you're actually saying "I admire you doing that," whereas the others are a form of action.

Last but not least, love. No matter what happens or goes on within a family, whether it is good or bad, love will prevail. It always does, because all the events you go to when you're mad, you go because they're family and you really do love them. So as we all know, love creates us to say things we don't necessarily mean, and things we do mean that also cause us to do things in the same respect. Because they're your family and no matter what you love them, that's why we do the things we do.

For my closing I would just like to say no, I haven't touched on all the aspects of families, I realize that there are so many things that happen or don't happen. I just want to say that no matter what, family is the most important thing, and eventually we all get through the hard times and work things out.

So when you are walking and you come across a homeless person, a bum, or a child on the street, just look back and thank everyone for being there for you, because no matter what happens your family will be there when you need them to be. It just takes time sometimes. But eventually it will happen. So remember to look outside the box, and you should see something blooming eventually. Just remember this. "We always realize what we have or had after we've lost it," and always tell them you love them, because you never know when you won't be able to anymore. Nobody needs any more regrets than he or she may already have, so why create more if it is at all avoidable?

Kids

This is going to be about kids, and even though I may not include men a lot in these writings, I will mention them periodically and then at the end I will write something about the role men play and some of the emotions they go through as well, so don't think I don't realize they are involved. After all it takes twenty-three chromosomes from each person to make a baby, so please bear with me.

I also have to let you know that not every woman's pregnancy is the same. Some have more complications than others, some barely gain any weight, some are bedridden at an early stage, some are very athletic, some need vitamin supplements, some have the support of their whole family, including the man, some only have their families, some only have their friends, and sadly enough, some only have themselves. Some women also have pre-stress, and some have post-stress.

Although we all have different circumstances during the pregnancies, we all have the same emotions. And that is what I'm talking about with this.

So let's talk about kids. Oh my God! Where do we start?

Children are the only ones that can make us go through every emotion known to mankind. We go through the emotions from the time of conception right through the rest of their lives. Some of the emotions are:

Anxiety: This comes from waiting anxiously for the results of the in-home pregnancy test. Then we have panic, which happens when you find out that you are pregnant and you're not sure what you're going to do, or what the father of the child will say, or if he'll be happy about the pregnancy. Then comes excitement; that's when you realize you're really pregnant and you're going to have a baby. Then comes fear; that's as to whether or not you'll be a good mom, if you can give it everything it needs, and whether or not you're ready to even raise a child. Then the realization kicks in, and you just repeat the questions to yourself that you just asked.

So now that you've just experienced all of those and then some, here comes the morning sickness, which can actually happen morning, noon, and night.

With that comes your first stage of depression, which is the question "Is it ever going to come to an end?" or "I don't know if I can deal with this for the next eight months," and "Oh my God can this actually last the whole nine months?" Then the worry starts as in; your first doctor's appointment informs you how much weight you can gain and all the things you have to do to ensure a healthy baby. So you worry about eating right, not gaining too much weight, and exercising. You experience panic once again if the doctor tells you that you have a deficiency, but with the info you get from the doctor the panic goes away. Then you feel joy and excitement, because the doctor tells you when your first ultrasound will be and when they can tell you the gender of the baby. Then anticipation happens in waiting for that appointment. Then you get a little relief from your emotions because you're just waiting for the sickness to go away.

So as you can see, we've already gone through so many emotions it's unbelievable, and you're not even past your first month yet. So now that we've had a break and are going into the third month, things start happening again. You have already had several doctor's appointments. So now once again the excitement happens, every store you go into you end up in the baby section, you start looking at maternity clothes, you may even have to buy some depending on the person. You're also starting to check your stomach to see if it's getting bigger. And even though you don't realize it, a least once in every situation you're in, your hand will always end up in the vicinity of your stomach, whether it's just to rub it or to guard it in one way or another, and that is done instinctively.

Then we start to worry again, and if you are getting a tummy you might get a little paranoid about your weight. Not only that, but the cravings start, and you'll find then and later that you'll eat some very weird combinations, and you may not be able to eat the things you always loved to eat. Oh yes, I forgot to mention the mood swings. They usually only last as long as the sickness does, because it's all related to the change and adjustments that our bodies are going through to house the beautiful child you're carrying.

Mood swings are swift. One minute you're happy, then crying, then laughing, then screaming, and then you're fine. I know it's frustrating, confusing, and you just don't understand, which means you have more emotions to deal with. But luckily the people around us understand, so that's a big help. And even though you may not realize it, you will later on.

So now we're at a little more than five months. Here we go again—the excitement kicks in, and you're going to find out if it's a boy or girl. Some can't wait; others don't care as long as the baby is healthy and has all its fingers and toes. Remember, that's just a saying; for most that doesn't matter because it's theirs.

Just remember we're keeping this a healthy pregnancy. As I said earlier, there is the possibility that it isn't, and it depends on the problem where someone places blame for a problem, and yes that is a possible emotion. Just remember that anything genetic is not one person's fault if it happens and the person may not have known about it. So if you know of any, you are better off telling the other person so blame cannot come into the picture.

So now we are coming to around seven months, when you really start to show. Now the fun begins, because all of the old feelings and insecurities start flooding back. Now only real emotion that is prominent is the excitement, because you are bigger, and the baby is already active. And boy, can they kick hard or what. Some can kick so hard that they kick your partner right out of bed, like my son did. Oh, by the way, that was very painful for me as well.

So now we go through the stage of Lamaze class, which seems silly at first but believe me, when you're having the baby you'll be thankful you went to those classes. For the rest of the time your emotions might go a little crazy, but as the days go by your excitement and anticipation grows, and then all of a sudden its time and hopefully it's a natural child birth. With a cesarean section you don't experience the pain or anything, but what they don't tell you is that you experience natural child birth after, and believe me, I'll take natural first. It almost seems easier to get rid of all the excess weight when it's natural rather than cesarean. I can say this because I had three natural child births and one cesarean, and it seemed to take forever to lose the weight after the cesarean. And yes, the cesarean pain afterwards was very intense, so I speak from experience.

So now you've had the baby and it's beautiful. It's so exciting; you just can't wait to show everyone your beautiful child. So you get home and you start not getting any sleep because the baby wakes up in the middle of the night. Then exhaustion kicks in, followed by lack of energy, impatience, and even anger. And that's all okay, it's a normal process, but usually depression comes as well. It's called postpartum depression, and believe me you want to make sure you are in contact with people during this because then it won't be so bad, and it won't take as long to run its course. Believe it or not it can take years for this to go away, that's why they have society out there to help. Know that you are not any less a mom for seeking help. If anything, it makes you a better mother because you noticed the problem and got help before anything happened.

Just remember, a lot of us have gone through the first pregnancy and we all need help, so just ask. After all, people love to give advice, and when it comes to kids everyone has an opinion. The trick is to pick which piece(s) of advice suits you best. Just remember you're not alone. Yes, although people have lots of friends and family to help them they can still get the feeling of being alone, but everyone goes through it, you really aren't the only one.

All through a child's growing life you are going to go through each and every emotion I've mentioned, so now I'm just going to write about kids and the pleasures and some of the not so pleasant experiences of raising them. As you are reading, you'll be able to notice the different emotions mentioned. The answer is to notice them and to correct any bad ones we may end up having. We have all heard of things that have happened to children due to our emotions getting the best of us, so I figure that maybe by me putting them in a book where you can read about it, maybe it'll help you see the beginnings of these, and you can deal with them appropriately. Always remember that you're not alone.

I find that a child from the ages of six months to five to six years old can turn the meanest and most grumpy person into a big sap. I say those ages because before they are six months people think they are breakable, which is true, but they are not as breakable as we think, they are born with things to help flexibility. They mostly just eat, sleep, and go to the bathroom, what's up with that? And after they are six years of age their little personalities aren't as cute as they once were, because adults think their cute personality is just an attitude, and they may not like that. Because, let's face it, some kids get quite the attitude, such as my youngest child. She was an attitude waiting for a place to happen, and even at twenty-six years old she still has the attitude.

But anyways, lets go back to the little ones and the pleasures we experience, such as their first smile, the first time they really focus on you, the grip they have when they hold one finger, that first real giggle, learning how to roll over, learning to crawl, their first step, and the first time they say "Mom" or "Dad". What I find amazing is how parents tell people when this all happens, the excitement in their voices is just so incredible, and every time a new parent tells you all about these great things you can't help but remember your own kids, the times when they did all these things and the joy and excitement you feel once again. The pride that people feel is also incredible. You can't help but feel proud as well, because they make it out like their child just conquered the world, and they sort of did, because it was their world they were conquering. This makes the child excited, which then causes even more excitement for you, and you just laugh, which is such a great feeling.

So while you are going through those feelings you forget about how much sleep you haven't had, you forget the times the baby was sick and wouldn't stop crying, or the dirty diapers and the throw up. It just seems so worth it when they are laughing, making new discoveries, and sleeping like angels. It is so amazing, because every child looks so much like an angel when they sleep.

But one process we all go through is trying to remember all those fairy tale stories you either read or were told as a child, or the little prayer you had, so you can teach your child as soon as they can speak well. During their sleeping hours we are given the opportunity to dream of what they'll be like when they get older. Then we think "for Pete's sake that's not for a long time," but in an instant you wake up and realize it'll be sooner than we think, and when the panic goes from thinking these thoughts we go back to dreaming of everything else. So even if you think you're not a dreamer any longer, you sure get that back fast once you have a child.

See, it's amazing the abilities kids have, and they don't even know it. But in fact we all have those abilities, it's just that as we grow and have our own experiences, we tend to forget our hopes and dreams and just plug along. So the sudden memory of our own childhood when our kids are born is not really too unbelievable.

The joy of having a child is more than most people without children will ever realize. As for Christmas day, that is truly the one day that everything a family member has done to you during the year or even earlier in the day doesn't matter, because of how grateful they are to you for the things they have and how much love they give to you. It's almost a feeling of inner peace, because you're relaxed, laughing, unstressed, and remembering all the real joy this person brings into your life, and how you wouldn't give that up for anything. It's just the greatest feeling ever, I'm sure most would agree.

So now the years are going by and your children start getting into all kinds of sports, dance, etc. And sometimes you don't really know how you're going to make these things possible, but you always do, and when you don't it is teaching them a valuable lesson. You'll tell them that, and they won't always understand. Then as they get older they start to be more fashion-conscious, but that's another story.

It's just through all this depending on your situation as to how much you can do for them, and even though sometimes you're not doing the best job, you are doing the best job you can. Once again there are people out there that can help; you just have to say something.

Kids also have a way of making you feel like you are doing a great job, because just out of the blue, they'll give you a handmade card, or a hug, or tell you they love you and maybe even help around the house. See, as we all know, kids have a sixth sense, they can pick up on any stress or something negative that's happening to you, and they'll do anything to give back the love you gave to them. That alone can make everything seem doable.

So remember, kids are not only your pride, joy, heart, and soul, but they can be your savior as well, so never under estimate the ability of a child, because when you do you both miss out.

Just remember, before they were born you called them your little miracle and looked at them always as such because they are, and they will always do things to confirm that as long as you always keep your eyes and mind open. Always remember the saying "children do as they are taught," so be careful as to what you teach them, because it may eventually bite you in the butt.

Now, as I stated at the beginning, I said I would talk about the role men play in all this. For the most part, men's role's in the upbringing of a child really start after the kids are five. This is because until then the mom usually teaches them social skills such as manners, most of the rights and wrongs, emotions, and sharing.

The man is there mostly for the woman, especially during the pregnancy. I really give a lot of credit to the man because of all the emotions that they have to endure during that time. For some they walk on eggshells the whole time. They not only deal with the emotions, but some hold your hair when you're sick, they get you drinks after it's all said and done, they'll run for the craving you are having, attend doctor appointments, and go to Lamaze even when they don't want to.

They are our rocks, and at the best of times we don't even realize it. And ladies, how often have you said to him "Thank you so much for everything you do and put up with." Really think about it. Most of the time this is the source of problems. The man should do all those things because it's his child too, it's not him going through the pain, and it's not his body that's getting ruined, what do you have to do but nothing?

But ladies, remember that they go through it as well by way of you. And sometimes they even go through pain, because usually the baby is mobile while you're sleeping, and you snuggle up to the man but the baby kicks the tar out of their back. So really think about it. You really aren't the only one that feels relieved when the baby is born, but he dare not say or at least say often that he'll be glad when the baby's born because he risks one of your bad emotions kicking in, and you taking a strip off him for it. But all through the pregnancy he's touching your stomach, talking to you, and most even talking directly to the baby. So when the baby is born, it will definitely recognize both voices.

So now he's made it through the pregnancies with not too many problems. Now it's after the baby is born and he's there to help with the baby, to make sure you all feel safe, and his biggest job is to make you feel attractive again, which can be very hard to do because we all get so paranoid about the weight we gained during the pregnancy. Shortly after the babies born he has all of the other emotions that you go through to get through himself, with both of you keeping your sanity and marriage intact.

So know this ladies; The one emotion that men go through is feeling like they are playing second fiddle to the baby, and although that seems ridiculous, you have to remember if you waited to have children after you either married or lived together, and if he had your undivided attention. Even though he doesn't understand it because it's his child as well, it's still a very real emotion men go through. They can't talk to us about it because it seems so ridiculous that we probably wouldn't understand, and for the most part men don't normally talk to other men about their feelings or emotions. They end up dealing with it on their own, which sometimes turns into be a big argument. Because of this we must realize that there are things our men deal with upon a new arrival that we have no clue about until it's too late, but now you have a head's up. Also this feeling they have can go all through the child's upbringing in the same way that your emotions do, so please keep these things in mind if he's acting very weird toward you and the baby. It's almost like a man's postpartum, which can also happen, by the way.

I say these things because they are the sort of things that don't usually get discussed when women get together.

So other than making sure the whole family is taken care of and protected as well, there isn't much the man has to do, other than playing ball and teaching the boy how to go the washroom the boy way. He does most of his work later on in life, and like I said that's another story.

So men really do deserve more credit than they get. I tip my hat to most men because they can be totally amazing during this time.

Although I may have said this already, I'm going to say it again. Children are little gifts and miracles, and they should always be treated as such.

Motherhood

I'd like to say something about motherhood. Some of these things I'm about to say will verify things you've said, heard, discussed, and even felt.

I don't have all the answers, and no, I'm not an expert by the sense of the word, and yes, I'm still trying to figure out different things I can do and different ways to deal with my kids on certain matters. But one thing I will tell you is that I haven't led a very comfortable life, I've had a lot of ups and downs, and my kids have been through an awful lot as well.

Over the last year or so I have come to a lot of realizations and realities of my life, and reflected on some of the things my own mother taught me that were things she did herself. So I am hoping that the things I have realized will help others.

I'd like to start by reiterating something we've all heard, which is; "Oh, when they turn eighteen then they get a job and go out on their own and that's it." Well, as most of us know that is not true, parenthood is a life sentence, especially for the woman because of her emotions. She feels more of the guilt and responsibility to her children than most men do. And I say most men because I know some men that feel and think the same way that most women do, but not every male parent has these feelings.

Although motherhood for the most part is the greatest feeling you'll ever have, it sure has its ups and downs, and it definitely causes us to question ourselves a lot. The gift of a child can be such a beautiful thing, but it can be just as devastating. The whole time we're raising our kids, all we can think of is giving them everything they want and need, and also making sure they have everything we didn't have. Sometimes it seems like no matter how hard we try, or what we do, it's not good enough. So then frustration and anger sets in, and we either say or do something our parents did; something that we swore we'd never do, and we beat ourselves up for it.

Much like men and women, kids don't come with a manual, though it make things so much easier. But they don't, so we either do what we think is the right thing or we do something that we don't think we have any other option to do, and when it doesn't work out, we beat ourselves up again. It is an ongoing process.

I realize that there a lot of books out there to help with some of the problems we encounter while raising kids, and in some situations they can definitely help. There are also friends and family, however, sometimes they have more opinions than helpful advice. After all, people always have lots to say when kids are concerned. For the most part, however, we feel more like they are judging our parental skills than helping. But the key is to remember that while they are telling us what we should do, they only mean well.

Motherhood is mostly filled with bliss, especially during the ages before the children are teenagers. Then after that, they really start trying our patience. Motherhood is definitely a challenge and a learning experience. For the most of us, we end up raising our kids like we were raised. Yes, of course there are specific things we told ourselves that we wouldn't do, but we change during the raising stages, because those were things that we didn't like our parents doing. Those things are the things that we have told ourselves just about every day while we were young, and also as adults. But there are things that we didn't like that we put far, far, into our thoughts, and every so often, they rear their heads and sends us for a whirl, which makes raising our kids even more difficult, because not only do we have to work on ourselves, but our kids as well if we see that its affected them badly. Then we start doubting ourselves and beating ourselves up, because that's not where you wanted to go with your kids, but the important thing is that you can see the problem, and therefore deal with and fix it. This can be an ongoing process, but at least you noticed it and can start the process to turn things around for everyone. We all do it at one time or another, so you should pat yourself on the back for having the realization and doing something about it, because it's one of the hardest things you can do, and that's to change an old habit.

Then after all that, we have to deal with our daughters' interest in boys, and trying our best to make sure that they only get together with good boys and that our daughters don't make the same mistakes we made. But you know what? Most of them will, and there is not much we can do. If you just let it go, then you're faced with the words "You don't care," but if you get a little overbearing then you end up pushing them away, and it's even worse. So basically, all we can do is make sure they know the facts of life and about the protection that's out there, and also we can give them advice, but try not to be to insistent or assertive. Instead just sit back and watch closely, no matter how much it drives them crazy, and be there to pick up the pieces, never saying "I told you so," or "If you would have just listened," because those words always bite you in the butt. Some phrases that have worked for me of with teenagers are "I'm not saying this to hear myself talk," or "I do have an idea what you're talking about, I was your age at one time," or "I only say these things so that maybe others won't do as I have. After all, look at me. I'm forty-six and still a waitress, do you want that for yourself?" For the most part, we get into more of a conversation and they ask questions, which is good.

The only thing is that with our own kids we can't be too much of their friend; we have to be just the right amount of being their parents, which can be hard and confusing. The most important thing is to be there when they make a mistake or fall, because you were young once, and you thought similar things about your parents as they think of you. So always try to be understanding, and just be there. They will make realizations as you did. It just takes time sometimes, as it did for all of us.

Right now I am forty-six and a half, and I have just realized in the last eleven and a half years some of the things and methods that my mom used, so you're never too old to learn. I have three living children; the oldest will be thirty and the youngest twenty-six, and I am still dealing with different things in my kids' lives, and different things that they are doing or have done, as well. While I am dealing with all that and their realizations, they are making me deal with some of my realizations as well. So see, it never stops at eighteen, but almost everybody knows that, don't they?

So, to move on, alcohol and drugs come into the picture. First alcohol, there are some parents that feel they would rather have their children drink at home where 1) they feel it's safer, and 2) they can keep an eye on them, but kids sometimes abuse a good thing. No matter what we always have to be careful as to what and how we do things. Because when that gets old or they get bored, or you start putting restrictions on them after a while, they will go elsewhere to drink. So be careful as to what and how you teach them. Remember, they do as they are taught and shown, even when they are at the age of making their own decisions. I'm not saying you shouldn't let them drink while in your care; after all, my mom let us drink at her house, but she left us alone. That was one mistake, but nobody ever got hurt, thankfully. It's just that everyone got bored and they drank because there were no limitations or supervision. Even if she would have shown her face just once or twice, it probably would have been different. Also, if limits are set it's better as long as they are done tastefully.

You know, for some reason we as adults feel that we shouldn't tell our kids what we did and how we did it while we were kids. I guess maybe that's why they don't think we've been there or done that, and instead think that we know nothing about what they're going through. After all, that is why kids always say "Well how would you know?" or "You don't understand." That's because we give them the impression that we were never kids, but maybe if we would have told them some of the stories about what we did when we were kids they would actually listen. It's not that we have to tell them all the details, we can pick and choose just like you do while talking to your parents about something you did that they didn't known about. Believe it or not, kids do pay attention when you reminisce about time spent with your friends. We always think they are not within hearing distance when we start reminiscing; that is, until they say to us, "but you did this when you were a kid," and we reply with "How do you know that?" They say "Well, I heard you talking about it with our friends," and just when we think they never listen to a thing we say, it seems like they listen to just the wrong things sometimes.

After all, we all do have some great memories of what we did growing up; especially when we thought our parents didn't know. Today we all sit around either in the kitchen, living room, rumpus room, or even the garage and talk about the difference between when we were kids and how kids are today. So maybe if we shared a little more and emphasized on how safely we played, maybe they would do the same, or at least think more about what exactly they are doing.

So now an even scarier topic, and that's drugs. What can I say? The main thing you can do is realize that it is a definite possibility that they are going to experiment. Let your children know you realize it, and give them the information needed, especially nowadays. One of the keys is to let them know you're not going to judge them, and that you're there for them if they need you to be. Let them know they can talk to you. If they know that you trust their judgment and that you'll be there for them if they get carried away, they will come to you to help them through it, and you won't freak. You will understand, because even you may have tried drugs at one time, if you did, it will be that much easier when it all happens. Most importantly, don't make judgment.

I say this because one of my children got badly into the drugs, and it got so bad she tried to OD, and the only thing I could do was to be there when she needed me. No matter how much I didn't understand why she was doing what she did.. It was so frustrating, and it hurt, but I had to be strong for her through all the years, and there were a few, but it all worked out. So yes, I've been there, I've experienced it. It's hard, but everyone gets through it, and yes, it helps to remember the things they did as children that make you laugh, feel proud, and love them the way you do, because you can only cry and blame yourself for so long and to a certain degree.

So the last thing that we find hard to deal with is finding out one of our children is gay. Well it's quite a shock, but depending on what's going on sometimes it's more of a relief to find out that a child is gay than to get a phone call from the police or a visit from them saying that your child is dead and it happened through a drug overdose in an alley somewhere, or that they were brutally killed in another way. I know I've experienced that as well. Believe me, it's not all bad. . Gay couples have the same problems in their relationships as they would in an opposite sex relationship. So really sit back and just accept it, after all, they are your kids, and no matter what you will always love them. You may not always understand them, but they say the same things about us. So enjoy and treasure the time you have with them, because you never know when you won't be able to anymore.

I had four kids; one passed away just before her twenty-third birthday and believe me, it hurts, so take it from someone with experience. There are always going to be differences between you and your kids, but there are always ways to get through it, no matter what. Sometimes it takes time and a whole lot of patience, but remember that time is limited. Unfortunately, we always need an awakening to that. So once again, time is limited, but no matter what we always have patience. Sometimes our children like to try our patience, but it is something we'll always have. However, you may not always have your kids.

I only have a couple more things to add, and I do apologize if it seems like I left men out of the loop, but they have as much responsibility to children as women, it's just that women show their feelings and emotions a lot more. Being a woman, I tend to forget how many men I know personally that can express their feelings as much, and sometimes more than most women. So to all the men out there, I give my apologies. Remember, your job is to protect the children.

Always expect from your children the same as you expect from yourself. Expect them to do the best that they know how.

Remember, we are their teachers and their students, because we can learn as much from them as they can learn from us.

www.ingramcontent.com/pod-product-compliance
Lightning Source LLC
Chambersburg PA
CBHW031330290526
45784CB00014B/2463